CONTENTS

KV-510-427

INTRODUCTION

Things that happened years ago, way back in the mists of time, have had a huge influence on today's world. Wars have been lost and won, inventions have been, erm, invented, and science and medicine has come on in leaps and bounds.

Major events have happened throughout history because at some time, someone said: "Hmm. I think I may have a go at..." And then they had a go at something like building a pyramid or trying to split the atom, rather than putting their feet up and having a mug of cocoa.

But you don't need us to tell you how important history is. No doubt your teachers go on about it all the time. All those dates, all those battles, all those kings and queens you've got to remember.

HISTORY HOAXES

Tim Scott

Illustrated by Scoular Anderson

ISTE·IVSSIT· VTFO·D

Hodder

Text copyright 2000 © Tim Scott
Illustrations copyright 2000 © Scoular Anderson
Published by Hodder Children's Books 2000

Cover illustration by Kevin Jenkins
Book design by Don Martin

10 9 8 7 6 5 4 3 2 1

A catalogue record for this book is available from the British Library

ISBN 0 340 78320 6

Printed by The Guernsey Press Company Ltd, Guernsey,
Channel Islands

Hodder Children's Books
a division of Hodder Headline Limited
338 Euston Road
London NW2 3BH

Sometimes, just sometimes, the sheer excitement of history can get lost along the way. Well, this book is here to save the day! *History Hoaxes* will help liven up your history learning by injecting a bit of much-needed humour!

History Hoaxes is packed with well-researched, carefully documented evidence about historical events that is all COMPLETELY MADE UP. We have spent hours cross-checking and double checking to make sure that down to the tiniest detail the facts on all the right-hand pages are utter rubbish. We have sifted through piles of previously unexamined material and forgotten archives to make sure everything in these hoaxes is A LOAD OF WALLY.

Why on earth have we done that you may ask? Simple. So you can fool your teacher big time!

We all know that teachers just love historical documents...

But now's your chance to use this peculiar trait to your own advantage!

HOW TO USE THIS BOOK

- Choose a topic that you have been talking about at school (eg. the First World War).

- On the left-hand page is the Fast Fact File of true facts. All the information on the left-hand pages is completely true – you'll recognise a lot of the information from your history lessons. On the right-hand page is the hoax.

- Cut out the right-hand page.

- Make it look old (see tips on pages 22, 74 and 94).

- Show your teacher. If they believe it, you have fooled them BIG TIME!

Useful tip:
As you will by now be aware, this form of history hoaxing involves cutting up your prized possession – this book. I'd suggest that you read the whole book before cutting it up. That way you'll not only get your money's worth, but you'll be able to choose your favourite hoaxes to play on your teacher! Of course, another option would be to buy another copy of the book. But then I would say that, wouldn't I?

ANCIENT HISTORY
(up to 500 AD)

When Britain Was Very Muddy

The history of Britain can be measured in all sorts of
ways. By its art. By its literature. Or as I prefer, by its
mud. The further back in time we go – the more mud.

This time line explains the mud theory:

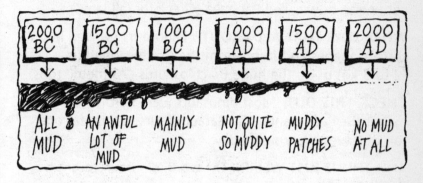

As you can see, the future will see mud dying out all
together. There will have to be special mud sanctuaries
where mud is preserved so it does not become extinct.
From here, mud will probably be released back into the
wild to re-establish itself in its natural habitat.

And so we come to Ancient History. Think back in
time. Think back, back, back. Think even further back.
Keep going back. Now stop. Forward a touch. Stop.
There. You are now back in the period some historians
call 'The Time of Ancient History'. The period up until
500 AD. A time of ancient civilisations, ancient peoples
and ancient...er...other things.

Put on your toga! Crown yourself with olive
branches! Cover your face in make up! Then take it all
off in case you get arrested. Behold – the ancient world!

DINOSAURS

WHEN? They lived 230 to 65 million years ago.

WHERE? At that time the earth had just one super-continent, now called Pangaea (Greek for 'all land').

WHAT WAS THAT ALL ABOUT? Dinosaurs evolved into all sorts of shapes and forms from the Compsognathus (2 to 3 kg) up to the huge Brachiosaurus (73 metric tons).

CHECK THIS OUT: Most dinosaurs were herbivores, which meant they ate plants. The Baraoposaurs had to eat one ton of leaves every single day.

AND THIS IS JUST WEIRD: The word 'dinosaur' means 'terrible lizard' in Greek.

HUMUNGOUS HOAX

Originally palaeontologists (those who study the geological past) thought that the Stegosaurus looked very different. This note shows what they thought it looked like.

The Science Museum
London SW1

Professor E. Burrows
Resident Professor of Palaeontology
Visiting Professor of Archaeology

Monday 30th July 1908

Dinosaur: Stegosaurus

We believe that the recently discovered bones of the Stegosaurus were from a prehistoric animal of the following proportions:

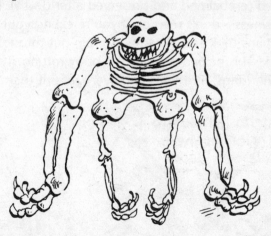

EGYPTIAN PYRAMIDS

WHEN? Most date from the Old Kingdom (approximately 2686-2181 BC).

WHERE? The west bank of the River Nile in modern Egypt, Africa.

WHAT WAS THAT ALL ABOUT? The Egyptian pyramids were built in honour of their dead pharaohs (rulers) and closest relatives. They had burial chambers nearby.

CHECK THIS OUT: In 1922, Englishman Howard Carter discovered the tomb of pharaoh Tutankhamun, (reigned 1361-1352 BC). Tutankhamun had a solid gold coffin. It is one of the few tombs ever to have been found that had not been ransacked by grave robbers.

AND THIS IS JUST WEIRD: Tutankhamun's body had been mummified (embalmed and preserved after death). It was a messy business – don't read on if you're eating your dinner. The Egyptians took Tutankhamun's brain out through his nose – yuk! This helped prevent the body rotting. They also took out his lungs, intestines and liver and put them in jars.

HUMUNGOUS HOAX

The Egyptian Pyramids were not originally intended to be
the shape they are. The following scroll shows some
alternative designs.
A 1920s Egyptologist has translated the hieroglyphics
alongside the pyramid as:
'The round one is good – but I like this one the best.
Tutankhamun.'

STONEHENGE

WHEN? The large standing stones date from 2100 BC. The circle of 30 stones was put up around 2000 BC.

WHERE? Stonehenge is 8 miles north of Salisbury, England.

WHAT WAS THAT ALL ABOUT? Nobody actually knows. The stones roughly line up with the direction of the sunrise on the longest day of the year (21st June), so it may have been used as a calendar.

CHECK THIS OUT: The stones for the main circle were transported about 20 miles from the Marlborough Downs. The large rougher standing stones were somehow brought from the Preseli Mountains of south west Wales.

AND THIS IS JUST WEIRD: Stonehenge is not believed to have been built by Druids, but nowadays many Druids go there on 21st June to celebrate the longest day.

HUMUNGOUS HOAX

What archaeologists now think Stonehenge originally
looked like before it fell down.

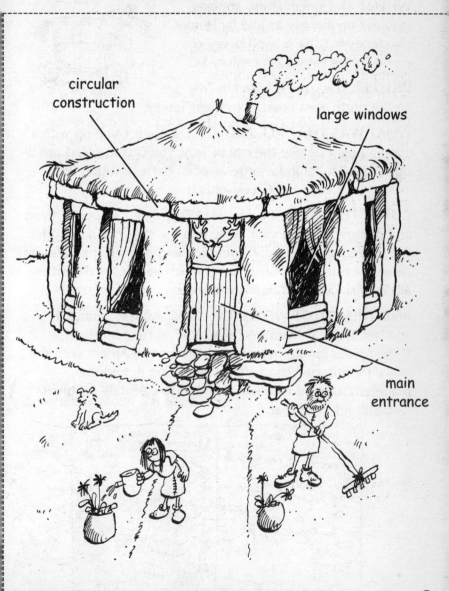

circular construction

large windows

main entrance

THE TROJAN HORSE

WHEN? The Trojan Horse appears in Greek mythology as told by Homer. His stories may have been based on events in the early 12th century BC.

WHERE? The story is based in Troy, on the north west coast of modern Turkey.

WHAT WAS THAT ALL ABOUT? Odysseus came up with a cunning plan to take the city of Troy. The Greeks sailed out of sight, but left behind a large wooden horse as a gift. But inside was a squad of Greek soldiers.

CHECK THIS OUT: The people of Troy didn't suspect a thing and dragged the wooden horse into the city. When night fell the soldiers sneaked out from inside and opened the gates. In came the rest of the Greek army which had not really left at all. They slaughtered nearly everyone.

AND THIS IS JUST WEIRD: The Greeks were victorious in another battle at Marathon in 490 BC. A runner called Pheidippides ran 26 miles from Marathon to Athens with the news. He dropped dead after announcing it, and the marathon running race was invented to celebrate his great feat with his great feet.

HUMUNGOUS HOAX

Before the success of the Trojan Horse, the Greeks had tried other Trojan animals which did not work – The Trojan Ant, The Trojan Moose and The Trojan Fish. This document illustrates their ideas.

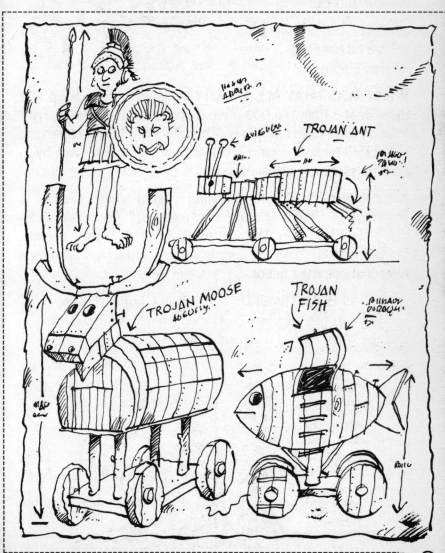

FAST FACTS FILE

ROMAN LEGIONS

WHEN? The Roman legion was fully developed by around 300 BC.

WHERE? Legions were posted all over the Roman Empire.

WHAT WAS THAT ALL ABOUT? A legion was made up of a division of 3,000 to 6,000 men. It consisted mainly of heavy infantry (also called 'hoplites' – heavily-armed foot soldiers), supported by light infantry (velites), and sometimes also by cavalry (soldiers on horseback).

CHECK THIS OUT: When fighting massed armies, the hoplites had a tactic of using a 'tortoise shell' formation. This was a square of men. Those at the front held up their shields in front of them, and the people in the middle held up their shields above their heads.

AND THIS IS JUST WEIRD: The hastati (youngest men) were at the front, the principes (seasoned troops) behind them, and the triarii (oldest men) were at the back.

I've suddenly got a nasty feeling that he may have said 'Christians fighting lions'.

HUMUNGOUS HOAX

As well as the 'tortoise shell' formation, this page from Professor Elgin's book proves that the armies often adopted alternative formations.

A HISTORY OF THE ROMAN ARMY
by Professor Elgin

The Roman Legions sometimes employed the 'tortoise shell' formation in battle:

However, they had other formations ready if that did not work. These were the 'snake' formation:

And the 'giraffe' formation.

HANNIBAL

WHEN? Hannibal, the
Carthaginian general,
was born in 247 BC.

WHERE? Carthage, a city on the Tunisian coast of
North Africa. It was a major Mediterranean power in
ancient times.

WHAT WAS THAT ALL ABOUT? Hannibal, one of the
world's greatest soldiers, started the Second Punic War (218-
201 BC) which was fought between Carthage and Rome.

CHECK THIS OUT: Hannibal planned to win the war by a
surprise invasion of Italy from the north. In 218 he led an
army of 30,000 up the Rhône River (which flows through the
Swiss Alps and part of France). Despite the distance and
snow, Hannibal's army succeeded in crossing the Alps, with
the help of elephants to carry food and equipment.

AND THIS IS JUST WEIRD: Hannibal was the eldest son of
Hamilcar Barca, who made 10-year-old Hannibal swear
eternal hatred of Rome.

HUMUNGOUS HOAX

Hannibal crossed the Alps by elephant, but not as a great tactical manoeuvre. It was because they were being chased by a mouse, and elephants hate mice. This extract from Hannibal's diary explains what happened.

Thursday, July 14th

Still the terrified elephants run from the mouse. It has been three days now and the mouse is starting to gain on us. There is nothing we can do except cling to the elephants as they stampede towards the mountains. As I stare back at the mouse with his little whiskers and see the determination in his eyes, I fear we will all perish. We have dropped all the supplies of cheese we can find, but the mouse has not been tempted. We have also tried hours of going "meeeow" in the hope he will think a cat is nearby — but the plucky mouse is not so easily fooled.

QUEEN BOUDICCA

WHEN? She was Queen of
the Iceni tribe around 61 AD.

WHERE? In present-day
Norfolk, England.

WHAT WAS THAT ALL ABOUT?
The queen's husband, Prasutagas,
died in 60 AD. He left his property to be divided among his
daughters and the Roman emperor. But the Romans took the
whole lot.

CHECK THIS OUT: Queen Boudicca got an army together
and caught the Romans off guard. She took Colchester,
killing every Roman she could find. She also attacked London
before Roman legions came down from the north and
defeated her.

AND THIS IS JUST WEIRD: Boudicca probably killed herself
with poison.

Queen Boudicca is revolting, sir.

You think so? I think she's rather nice.

HUMUNGOUS HOAX

Boudicca did not defeat the Romans with tactical skill and ferocity. She did it by shouting: "You're all just wearing sheets! Togas are just sheets!" until the Roman commanders were so embarrassed they ran away.

REPORT FROM CALIGULOUS, FEATURED IN THE BRITISH SECTOR

HAIL CAESAR!

QUEEN BOUDICCA DESCENDED ON CHELMSFORD LAST NIGHT AT LIGHTNING SPEED CAREERING THROUGH THE STREETS IN HER CHARIOT CRYING OUT THAT WE ARE ALL JUST WEARING SHEETS. THAT OUR TOGAS – THESE BEAUTIFUL TOGAS – ARE NOTHING BUT SHEETS SWOOPED ROUND US. AND I FEAR SHE IS RIGHT. OUR TOGAS ARE JUST WHITE SHEETS. I HADN'T THOUGHT ABOUT THAT BEFORE. THE MEN ARE BEGINNING TO FEEL A BIT SILLY. AND TODAY, ONE CAME TO DINNER IN SHORTS AND A T-SHIRT. IF IT GETS OUT TO THE REST OF THE EMPIRE THAT WE ARE JUST WEARING SHEETS, IT WILL BE THE END OF US – ROME WILL BE A LAUGHING STOCK.

ALL POWER TO THE GODS.

CALIGULOUS.

PS. PLEASE SEND MORE LEGIONS TO QUELL THIS UPRISING AND ALSO SOME TROUSERS.

HOAX TIPS (1)

All the documents in History Hoaxes look authentic, but with a little effort you can make them look very old indeed. Top Tip: try this out with an old sheet of paper first, before you use a page from the book.

You will need:
- ◆ This book
- ◆ Scissors
- ◆ Old tea bags
- ◆ A tray

● Cut out the document you wish to use.

● Tear the edges a little. Scrunch it up into a ball and then flatten it out again.

● Lay it flat on a tray and 'paint' it all over using the old tea bags.

● Finally leave it out flat to dry. When dry it should look extremely old.

Things That Happened Next

(500 to 1900 AD)

The Age of Reason. The Age of Wonder.
The Age of Things Being Not Quite So Muddy.

At some time around 500 AD, Ancient History finished and no one knew what sort of history would happen next. In fact, all kinds of different periods of history came and went. The Age of Darkness, the Age of Reason, The Age of Wonder, The Machine Age...

As mud began to decline, so people had to spend less time cleaning it off their shoes, leaving them free to do other things, like paint the Mona Lisa (Leonardo Da Vinci, 1503-1506) or go on Crusades to the Holy Land (13th century).

Of course, it did take some time for mud to lessen. It was still really quite muddy around the 11th century – but the foundations had been put in place and by the 19th century, mud was a lot less common.

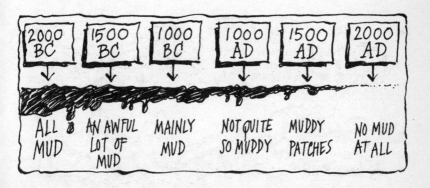

2000 BC	1500 BC	1000 BC	1000 AD	1500 AD	2000 AD
ALL MUD	AN AWFUL LOT OF MUD	MAINLY MUD	NOT QUITE SO MUDDY	MUDDY PATCHES	NO MUD AT ALL

The Legend of King Arthur

WHEN? Possibly based on a Saxon king from the 6th century AD.

WHERE? Camelot was King Arthur's castle and the home of the Knights of the Round Table. It has been suggested that it was either in modern day Winchester, England or Caerleon, Wales.

WHAT WAS THAT ALL ABOUT? In the legend, King Arthur and his knights woke up after a long sleep to rescue England in its darkest hour.

CHECK THIS OUT: The sorcerer Merlin was Arthur's tutor, but they never did maths or geography or anything like that. By pulling the sword Excalibur out of a rock, Arthur showed he was the true King of England.

AND THIS IS JUST WEIRD: The myth grew to include knights with the unlikely names of: Sir Tristram, Sir Bedevere, Sir Galahad, Sir Lancelot, Sir Gawain and Sir Percival.

HUMUNGOUS HOAX

King Arthur wasn't sure at first whether a round table was the best idea.

Camelot Furnishings
suggested designs for the King's meeting table:

King Arthur and the
Knights of...

the coffee table

the snooker table

the nest of tables

the triangular table

the round table

this one A. (King)

Castles

WHEN? Castles with a moat around them date from about the 9th century onwards.

WHERE? All over Europe.

WHAT WAS THAT ALL ABOUT? The people with the most power and money decided to build their own fortified dwellings.

CHECK THIS OUT: The Tower of London (built around 1078-97) is an example of the motte and bailey castle. Its White Tower is the original Norman keep.

AND THIS IS JUST WEIRD: With the invention of gunpowder, castles could be destroyed. Attacking artillery could fire cannon shot right into the heart of the castle.

HUMUNGOUS HOAX

Castle moats were not actually originally designed for defence, but for water sports such as diving and sailing. The drawbridge was raised so it did not interfere with the masts of the boats. The use of a moat as a defensive measure was only discovered later by accident.
This original drawing of an early castle and moat shows the real reason moats were dug.

Vikings

WHEN? Viking raids took place between AD 800 and 1100. The first recorded Norse raid in the British Isles was at Lindisfarne in 793.

WHERE? Lindisfarne (also called 'Holy Island') is off the coast of Northumbria in England. Vikings came from what is now Norway and Denmark.

WHAT WAS THAT ALL ABOUT? Using their sailing ships called longboats, Norse and Danish Vikings raided the coasts of Britain and France. As time went on, the raids got larger and more well organised.

CHECK THIS OUT: In the early 11th century, the Danish Vikings conquered all of England. The Danes gave two kings to England – Sweyn and Canute.

AND THIS IS JUST WEIRD: Important Viking chiefs were buried with their ships. One of these called *The Gokstad* was found in 1880 beneath a burial mound in southern Norway. It was 23 m long and 5.25 m wide.

I think it may need to be a touch bigger.

HUMUNGOUS HOAX

Why did the Vikings have such long boats? One reason was so that they could turn the boat into a bowling alley, play bowls and help pass the time during their long journeys at sea. This charcoal drawing excavated from a burial ground near Lindisfarne clearly shows the Vikings bowling on board one of their boats.

King Alfred 'the Great'

WHEN? Alfred was born in 849 and died in 899. He became king of Wessex in April 871.

WHERE? England. Wessex is what is present day south west England.

WHAT WAS THAT ALL ABOUT? Alfred was a great leader in war and fought the Danes from 876 until the end of his life. He also loved learning.

CHECK THIS OUT: Alfred wanted everyone to have the chance to read. He translated several books into Anglo-Saxon himself. These were *Pastoral Care* by Pope Gregory I, Orosius's *Seven Books of History Against the Pagans*, and *Ecclesiastical History* by the Venerable Bede.

AND THIS IS JUST WEIRD: Alfred was the only English king ever called 'the Great'.

HUMUNGOUS HOAX

King Alfred was keen to encourage everyone to learn to read when they weren't fighting the Danes. In fact he invented the first-ever reading card to help people understand the alphabet. This is the card.

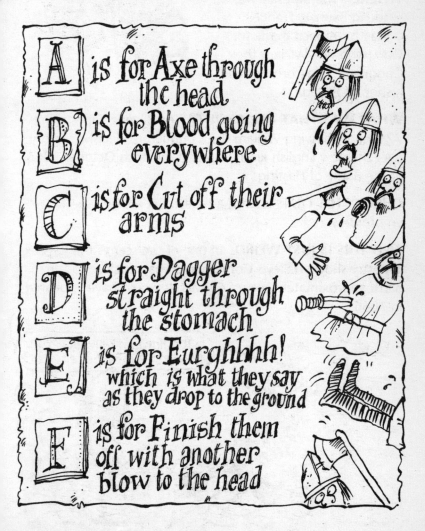

A is for Axe through the head

B is for Blood going everywhere

C is for Cut off their arms

D is for Dagger straight through the stomach

E is for Eurghhhh! which is what they say as they drop to the ground

F is for Finish them off with another blow to the head

The Bayeux Tapestry

WHEN? It probably dates from 1066 to 1077.

WHERE? The tapestry was made in Bayeux, France. It may have been made for Odo, who was William the Conqueror's half brother and bishop of Bayeux.

WHAT WAS THAT ALL ABOUT? The Bayeux Tapestry has 72 scenes showing William the Conqueror's decisive victory over the new English king, Harold II, on 14th October 1066 at the Battle of Hastings.

CHECK THIS OUT: It's not a tapestry at all, but an embroidery.

AND THIS IS JUST WEIRD: In one of the scenes the Bayeux Tapestry shows Halley's Comet which passes close to the earth approximately every 76 years. It would have appeared in 1066.

HUMUNGOUS HOAX

King Harold didn't actually get an arrow in the eye - he got some sand in it - thrown up by the Normans playing boules on the beach.

·1066· HASTINGS·

NB. To make this Hoax look authentic you'll need to embroider it. Stick it to a piece of material and use coloured wool to fill in different areas of the picture.

The Domesday Book

WHEN? The Domesday Book was completed in 1086.

WHERE? The book 'Great Domesday' covered all the counties except for Norfolk, Suffolk and Essex. These were covered later by 'Little Domesday'.

WHAT WAS THAT ALL ABOUT? It was a complete record of the English kingdom ordered by William the Conqueror. He wanted to know who owned what so he could work out how much to tax everyone.

CHECK THIS OUT: William sent people out all over the kingdom to collect the information, but the northernmost parts of England were never surveyed.

AND THIS IS JUST WEIRD: The name 'Domesday' was a reference to the Last Judgement. The reason was this – it was a census from which there was no appeal (escape).

HUMUNGOUS HOAX

William I did originally want the Domesday Book to include the north of England, but unfortunately the page was lost when the book was being compiled. It has since been recovered – here is the original page.

To William I, Conqueror of all England. Here be the findings of what be in the north of England, beyond the shires so far surveyed. This be a complete and full list of all that is there:

- 1 One twig.
- 1 A hill.
- 1 Another slightly smaller hill.
- 1 One hovel.
- 1 One peasant woman saying: "Ere, Harold – who's this on the horse?"
- 1 One man shouting: "Hello there – I hope you're not afraid of dogs?"
- 1 The same peasant woman saying: "Come and join us for a nice cup of broth, stranger."
- 1 The same man shouting: "Down Prince. Prince! Come back here!"
- 1 A large dog. (Extremely large and fierce with big teeth.)
- 1 Much barking.
- 1 Ripped clothing – in truth, my own.
- 1 Many more hills. (I did not have time to examine these because of the speed of my horse.)

I hope this is sufficient for your majesty. It is a wonderful place – incredibly beautiful. However, I regret I shall not be able to survey it further, as my horse is in need of a long holiday after his exertions.

Your humble servant John r Calwoon

The Hundred Years War

WHEN? 1294 to 1444.

WHERE? There were battles as far apart as Scotland (Battle of Bannockburn, 1314) and France (Battle of Crecy, 1346).

WHAT WAS THAT ALL ABOUT? It was partly over an area in south western France called Guienne, which the kings of England thought they had the right to rule. But the French did not like that. The French also supported the Kingdom of Scotland in its struggle against the English.

CHECK THIS OUT: The Hundred Years War actually lasted for 150 years.

AND THIS IS JUST WEIRD: The Battle of Crecy was won by the English – they had the advantage of archers armed with the longbow. Their arrows cut down the 15,000 mounted French knights. England had plenty of skilled archers because in 14th century England, it was the law that people should practise archery every Sunday.

HUMUNGOUS HOAX

Why was England always at war with France during this period (1294 to 1444)? The answer lies in the fact that the language spoken at court was French. Unfortunately, no one in England spoke French very well. This page from Edward II's French textbook shows he only learnt certain phrases. This meant that his court conversation was rather limited to declaring war.

LA FRANÇAIS POUR LES ROIX ET LES REINES   page 37

English	French Translation
I am King / Queen	Je suis le roi / la reine
I will cut your head off	Je vous trancherai la tête
Let's invade France / Scotland / Flanders	Nous allons envahi la France / l'Écosse / la Flandre
We will rule you	Nous allons régner

The Peasants' Revolt

WHEN? The largest Peasants' Revolt took place in 1381. The peasant army entered London on 13th June 1381.

WHERE? England. The main uprising was in the counties of Kent and Essex. But other smaller uprisings erupted throughout the countryside, particularly in Yorkshire, Cambridgeshire and Norfolk.

WHAT WAS THAT ALL ABOUT? It was mainly due to tax collectors trying to collect a new poll tax of a shilling a head. But its roots went back to the Black Death (1349) when so many people died there were not enough to work the land.

CHECK THIS OUT: The leaders Wat Tyler and John Ball took their army and entered London on 13th June 1381. Richard II met them on 14th June and granted their demands for the end of serfdom (serfs were labourers who were part of a lord's property and passed on to a new owner when the land was sold), the elimination of wage restrictions and low rents.

AND THIS IS JUST WEIRD: At a later meeting with the king, Wat Tyler was killed by the mayor of London. The rebels then dispersed and the king's concessions were all withdrawn.

Psst... I think you're on the wrong march.

BAN ALL FOX HUNTING

HUMUNGOUS HOAX

The real reason the Lord Mayor of London killed Wat Tyler at their second meeting was because they had a terrible misunderstanding about his name. Their conversation was recorded by the King's secretary...

The Secretary to his Majesty King Richard II.
The meeting between his Majesty the King,
The Lord Mayor of London and the rebels under the guidance of Wat Tyler. This is a full account of what was said betwixt the two - so help me God.

Lord Mayor: "Your name sir?"
Wat Tyler: "Wat."
Lord Mayor: "I said, your name sir?"
Wat Tyler: "Wat."
Lord Mayor: "What is your name?"
Wat Tyler: "Yes. Exactly sir."
Lord Mayor: "So what is it?"
Wat Tyler: "Yes. Wat."
Lord Mayor: "Look sir - I don't wish to play games. What is your name?"
Wat Tyler: "Wat indeed sir."
Lord Mayor: "Your name sir!"
Wat Tyler: "Are you deaf? Wat."
Lord Mayor: "What is this? I ask for your name!"
Wat Tyler: "Wat. Are you a complete imbecile?"
Lord Mayor: "I shall ignore that. I shall ignore that this time. But this is your last chance. Now, what is your name?"
Wat Tyler: "Wat. You stupid toad-faced idiot."

It was at this point that the Lord Mayor did stab and kill Mr Tyler.

The Mona Lisa

WHEN? Painted by Leonardo da Vinci between 1503 and 1506.

WHERE? It was painted in Florence, Italy.

WHAT WAS THAT ALL ABOUT? Also known as *La Gioconda*, the *Mona Lisa* is a portrait of the wife of Francesco di Bartolommeo del Giocondo di Zandi. No one can make up their mind whether she is smiling or not. Today it hangs in the Louvre in Paris.

CHECK THIS OUT: Leonardo was interested in many aspects of science as well. He made detailed plans of military weapons, fortifications, and paddle wheels amongst other things. He was also employed as a map maker and made discoveries in anatomy.

AND THIS IS JUST WEIRD: In one of Leonardo's notebooks is a drawing of what appears to be a helicopter – something that was not invented for another 400 years.

HUMUNGOUS HOAX

The Mona Lisa was reduced from its original size.
Quite often people did this to paintings when they didn't
have enough space to hang the entire picture.
The complete picture by Leonardo Da Vinci of
the Mona Lisa looked quite different:

King Henry VIII

WHEN? Henry VIII was king of England from 1509 to 1547.

WHERE? England, of course.

WHAT WAS THAT ALL ABOUT?

He was the second son of Henry VII, founder of the Tudor dynasty, and Elizabeth of York. When his older brother, Prince Arthur died in 1502, Henry became heir and succeeded his father in 1509.

CHECK THIS OUT: He had six wives – Catherine of Aragon (he divorced her) Anne Boleyn (he beheaded her), Jane Seymour (she died), Anne of Cleves (he divorced her), Catherine Howard (he beheaded her) and Catherine Parr (she survived). One way to remember this is with the little rhyme 'divorced, beheaded, died, divorced, beheaded, survived'.

AND THIS IS JUST WEIRD: Henry VIII was a talented musician and is thought to have written the tune *Greensleeves*.

HUMUNGOUS HOAX

Henry VIII had a seventh wife. To prove it here is the wedding invitation – the standard invitation he always used when marrying.

King Henry VIII of England

invites you to witness
the forthcoming marriage between
his Majesty and

~~Catherine of Aragon~~ ~~Anne Boleyn.~~
~~Jane Seymour~~ ~~Anne of Cleves.~~ ~~Catherine Howard.~~
~~Catherine Parr.~~ Catherine Anne Longneck.

at Hampton Court
on November 12th at half past 10 in the morning

Dress: Formal clothes with ruffs and puffy sleeves.

Jesters will be on hand to prance in the grounds.
More formal prancing and hopping will take place in
the Great Hall.

The Mary Rose

WHEN? Built in 1539 and sank in July 1545.

WHERE? Just off Portsmouth, England.

WHAT WAS THAT ALL ABOUT? It sank during action between the French and English fleets. The ship listed over possibly because she was top heavy – and the sea flooded in to her lower gun ports.

CHECK THIS OUT: She had sixty guns and an enormous crew of five hundred men. King Henry VIII watched her sink.

AND THIS IS JUST WEIRD: Two hundred years later another English ship – the *Royal George* sank in exactly the same way in exactly the same place.

HUMUNGOUS HOAX

The Mary Rose sank just outside Portsmouth Harbour. Historians thought this was possibly because she had too many guns on board and was top heavy. But the coastguard's original notes prove that it was because a perfect rainbow appeared on one side of the ship and all the crew ran over to have a look.

Portsmouth Coastguard Log Report

Year: **1545**
Ship lost: **The Mary Rose**
Survivors: **None**

The Mary Rose sank in a most unusual way just outside the confines of Portsmouth Harbour on this very day in July. She was in full sail in calm seas and in no difficulty when a rainbow appeared on her starboard side. Indeed it was a perfect one – so those on the starboard side called out to those manning the guns on the port side to come and look. All at once it seemed everyone on that ship rushed headlong to the starboard side lest they should miss seeing this vision. And the terrific weight of all crew being on the one side of the ship sent it first leaning and then toppling right over into the sea. I would not have believed such a thing could happen.

Witnessed by mine own eye on this day in July 1545.

E. Keele. Coastguard, Portsmouth Harbour

Elizabethan Ruffs

WHEN? Worn by the Elizabethans from around 1560.

WHERE? They originated in Spain but were quickly adapted all over Europe.

WHAT WAS THAT ALL ABOUT? Ruffs were a fashionable piece of clothing worn around the neck.

CHECK THIS OUT: After 1565, with the introduction of starch, ruffs became larger. They required expert laundering and had to be shaped when damp, using heated metal rods called 'poking sticks'.

AND THIS IS JUST WEIRD: The fashionable ruff gradually increased in size until 1580-85, when it extended nine inches on either side of the neck and each one was made of 18 yards of material.

Darling - we need a word with the carpenter.

HUMUNGOUS HOAX

Elizabethan ruffs were worn to stop animals going down your neck.

THE LATEST RUFFS
TO PREVENT MICE AND OTHER RODENTS GOING DOWN YOUR NECK

Slippery in the extreme. Surface not agreeable to mice and rat claws.

Fully starched ruffs and wrist ruffles. Guaranteed for six minutes.

Tight fitting to stop small mice.

The Spanish Armada

WHEN? 30th July 1588.

WHERE? Just off Plymouth.

WHAT WAS THAT ALL ABOUT?
The Armada was a Spanish
fleet assembled in 1588 as
part of the attempt by Philip II
to invade England. It was met by an English fleet under the
command of the captains Francis Drake, Martin Frobisher and
John Hawkins (Drake's cousin).

CHECK THIS OUT: Sir Francis Drake was playing bowls on
Plymouth Hoe when he heard the Armada had been sighted.

AND THIS IS JUST WEIRD: He is supposed to have finished
his game before going to engage the enemy.

HUMUNGOUS HOAX

Drake hated losing and was being beaten solid by Martin Frobisher and John Hawkins. Below is the bowls score card from that day.

PLYMOUTH HOE DISTRICT
PUBLIC BOWLS

Rules: Players must wear soft shoes and frilly ruffs around their necks. All swoopy-shaped captains' hats must be left in the pavilion. Any sea captains breaking the rules will be asked to leave.

PLAYER	SCORES						
Francis Drake	0	0	0	0	0	0	0
Martin Frobisher	1	0	3	1	2	0	2
John Hawkins	2	3	0	2	1	3	1

Martin — Francis is so bad at this game but won't give up until he wins. I think we'll have to lose the next game on purpose or the Spanish will invade — John.

Sir Walter Raleigh

WHEN? Sir Walter Raleigh was born around 1552, and executed in 1618.

WHERE? He was executed at the Tower of London, England.

WHAT WAS THAT ALL ABOUT? Although a favourite courtier of Elizabeth I from about 1581 until her death in 1603, he fell into serious disfavour when James I came to the throne, and spent 13 years locked up in the tower until 1616.

CHECK THIS OUT: In 1616 he persuaded James I to let him go on an expedition to find gold and the lost city of El Dorado in South America. However, he became involved in military action with the Spanish, and when he returned empty handed he was executed on a charge of conspiracy.

AND THIS IS JUST WEIRD: Raleigh introduced tobacco and pipe smoking to Great Britain in 1586. He is also credited with bringing the first potatoes to England.

HUMUNGOUS HOAX

Everyone knows that Sir Walter Raleigh laid his cloak down in a puddle so Queen Elizabeth I would not get her feet wet. What many people don't know is what happened next.

THE LONDON TIMES

15th May 1584

PEASANT RAMPAGE

A NUMBER of peasant farm labourers marched into London yesterday, demanding better working conditions and more pay. However, the self-appointed Minister of Agriculture Sir Wilberforce Crawley confronted them and requested that they stop making such a fuss and instead work harder and plant more crops for the growing population.

The farm labourer's union leader is said to be 'disgusted and disappointed' at the lack of support and is understood to be planning strike action.

QUEEN IN AIR

Sir Walter Raleigh – favourite of her Majesty Queen Elizabeth I caused a great storm by his actions today. First, he laid his cloak down over a puddle so her Majesty did not get her feet muddy. But when her Majesty stepped on to the cloak he withdrew it sharply sending her sprawling into the air. He apologised later to her Majesty, but it is reported he has still not stopped laughing.

A MIDSUMMER NIGHT'S DREAM

COME and see William Shakespeare's exciting new play! Described as 'lighthearted, entertaining and one for all the family', *A Midsummer Night's Dream* is being performed at 'The Player's Theatre' in Old Town, London and has an all star cast. There are two performances daily, between May 30th and June 21st, after which it goes on tour to the provinces.

51

William Shakespeare

WHEN? William Shakespeare was
born in 1564 and died in 1616.

WHERE? Born in
Stratford-upon-Avon,
Warwickshire, Shakespeare
lived and worked in London.

WHAT WAS THAT ALL ABOUT?
He wrote 36 plays, 154 sonnets, (a kind of poem) and 2
narrative poems. They are the most widely admired pieces
of literature by anybody in the history of our western
civilisation.

CHECK THIS OUT: Shakespeare wrote his plays just for his
own theatre company, at the rate of about two a year. In
1599, his theatre company built and ran the Globe Theatre
in London.

AND THIS IS JUST WEIRD: Some historians don't believe
Shakespeare actually wrote the plays at all, but claim they
were written by another playwright called Christopher
Marlowe, or even by the courtier Sir Philip Sidney.

Oh really, Will—
you can't get
writer's block
over a shopping
list!

HUMUNGOUS HOAX

William Shakespeare had a lot of trouble coming up with the idea for his play 'Romeo and Juliet'. This is the original parchment, showing all the other titles he thought up for it first.

Titles for a new play

Romeo and something, er...

~~Romeo and A Small Animal with a Long Snout~~

Romeo and A Shopping Bag

Romeo and My Auntie Enid

Romeo and The Case of The Thousand Knives

Romeo and His New Shed

Romeo and a Very Large Halibut

Romeo and Basil

Romeo and Herbert

Romeo and Derek

Romeo and John

Romeo and Juliet

Oliver Cromwell

WHEN? Oliver Cromwell was born in 1599, and died in 1658. In December 1653, after the execution of King Charles I and the collapse of the government, Oliver Cromwell became Lord Protector of England, Scotland and Ireland.

WHERE? He was based in London, England.

WHAT WAS THAT ALL ABOUT? It happened after King Charles I was defeated in the English Civil War, which started in 1642. The House of Commons felt the King was too powerful and they were particularly angry when Charles I raised new taxes without asking them. Oliver Cromwell was a military commander for Parliament. Their army was nicknamed the Roundheads. The King's army was known as the Cavaliers.

CHECK THIS OUT: In 1657 Parliament offered to make Oliver Cromwell king. He refused the offer.

AND THIS IS JUST WEIRD: He died in 1658 and was buried with pomp and ceremony in Westminster Abbey. However, in 1660 Charles II was crowned as king. The son of Charles I, he ordered Oliver Cromwell's corpse to be dug up, hanged, and then beheaded.

1 Squareheads
2 Roundheads
3 Extremely Elongated Heads

So we've narrowed down the choice. Those in favour of squareheads?

HUMUNGOUS HOAX

The Cavaliers wore big flouncey hats which did not give any protection, unlike the Roundheads' helmets.
The reason was because King Charles I mistakenly thought more people would join his army if he offered them a more exciting uniform. So he designed the hat himself. Here is the original document.

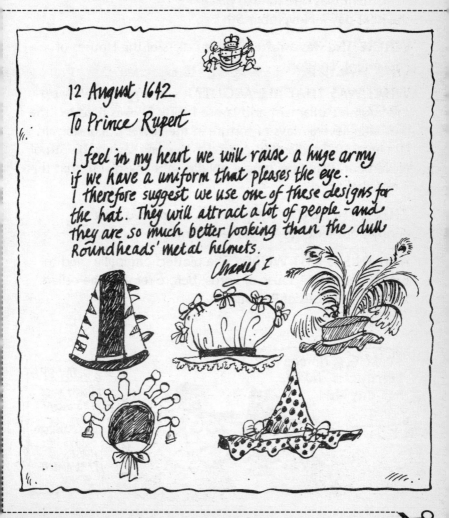

12 August 1642

To Prince Rupert

I feel in my heart we will raise a huge army if we have a uniform that pleases the eye. I therefore suggest we use one of these designs for the hat. They will attract a lot of people - and they are so much better looking than the dull Roundheads' metal helmets.

Charles I

FAST FACTS FILE
Gunpowder Plot

WHEN? On 4th November 1605, Guy Fawkes was arrested surrounded by barrels of gunpowder. The opening of parliament was due to take place the next day – November 5th.

WHERE? He was arrested in the cellars of the Houses of Parliament, London.

WHAT WAS THAT ALL ABOUT? It was a plot to blow up the English Parliament and James I. Guy Fawkes revealed the plot after several days of torture in the Tower of London. In January 1606 parliament passed a new law saying the 5th of November would become a holiday in thanksgiving that the plot failed.

CHECK THIS OUT: The plan was uncovered by an anonymous letter to the government.

AND THIS IS JUST WEIRD: The plotters originally tried to tunnel under the House of Lords, before renting the cellars under the Houses of Parliament.

HUMUNGOUS HOAX

Guy Fawkes was arrested in 1605 in the cellars of the Houses of Parliament, allegedly surrounded by barrels of gunpowder. However, he wasn't intending to blow up Parliament at all. It wasn't gunpowder in those barrels. It was powdered soup. Guy Fawkes was planning to sell hot soup to everyone going into the Houses of Parliament the next day. After all, it was November.
This poster has recently come to light.

Fawkes - Where Taste Talks

Guy Fawkes will be selling hot soup from piping hot barrels in the cellars under the Houses of Parliament on November 5th.

Flavours	Eat in cost	Take out cost	Hover in the doorway cost
Potato and Leek	2d	1d	$1^1/_2$d
Carrot and Rat	2d	1d	$1^1/_2$d
Fish and More Fish	2d	1d	$1^1/_2$d
Turnips	2d	1d	$1^1/_2$d

For Soup That's Hot

For Taste That Talks

For all your soup - just ask GUY FAWKES!

The Great Plague

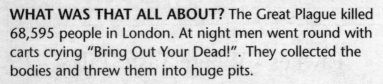

WHEN? It began in
December 1664, and carried
on through 1665.

WHERE? London was badly hit,
but it spread throughout the
whole of England, wiping out whole villages.

WHAT WAS THAT ALL ABOUT? The Great Plague killed
68,595 people in London. At night men went round with
carts crying "Bring Out Your Dead!". They collected the
bodies and threw them into huge pits.

CHECK THIS OUT: Nobody knew how the plague spread.
The government ordered all dogs to be killed thinking they
might be the cause. Dog killers were paid 1d for each dog
they killed.

AND THIS IS JUST WEIRD: When a person died of plague,
the house they were from was marked with a red cross on
the door and no one (except a doctor) was allowed in or out
for forty days.

HUMUNGOUS HOAX

Once a house was marked with a cross you knew someone had died of plague there. But there were other marks used on the doors at this time too. Samuel Pepys describes them in his famous diary.

Once a house was marked it meant that no one could go in or out for forty days. These were the marks I saw about London.

A red cross on the door meant someone in the house had died of plague.

A circle on the door meant that someone in the house had not had a bath for over five years.

A triangle on the door meant someone in the house had picked their nose in public.

The Great Fire of London

WHEN? September 2nd 1666.

WHERE? It started in a bakery in Pudding Lane, London.

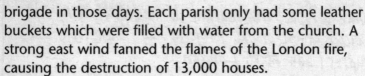

WHAT WAS THAT ALL ABOUT? There was no London fire brigade in those days. Each parish only had some leather buckets which were filled with water from the church. A strong east wind fanned the flames of the London fire, causing the destruction of 13,000 houses.

CHECK THIS OUT: Charles II joined the fire-fighters himself and ended up blackened by smoke and soaked in water. He ordered whole rows of houses to be blown up with gunpowder to stop the fire spreading. Afterwards he appointed Sir Christopher Wren to rebuild London.

AND THIS IS JUST WEIRD: The people of London blamed French spies for starting the fire and attacked Frenchmen in the streets. In fact, a Frenchman called Robert Hubert even confessed to starting the fire and was hanged, although he wasn't even in London at the time. Weird.

HUMUNGOUS HOAX

The Great Fire of London was not started by accident in a bakery in Pudding Lane. It was started on purpose, not by French spies - but by Sir Christopher Wren.

It appears that Christopher Wren started many fires throughout London at this time, the one of 1666 being the largest. This ensured that he would get plenty of work afterwards, building new churches and cathedrals. Indeed, after the 1666 fire he was commissioned to build the fabulous St Paul's Cathedral (1675–1710).

Samuel Pepys wrote a famous diary at the time. This extract provides conclusive evidence.

4th September 1666

I dare not breathe it - but it is being said about London that this Great Fire did not start by accident in a bakery in Pudding Lane but that it was started on purpose by the architect Mr Wren. In the past few weeks I myself have unexpectedly come across Mr Christopher Wren with matches and bits of paper crouched down in alleyways and muttering to himself 'Burn! Come on burn! Oh for crying out loud. Burn!" And when I did approach him to ask about what he was doing, he would rise quickly and say he had been tying up his shoe. Meanwhile, he would be hastily throwing the matches away behind his back. I did not know what to make of it ~ but now I think he had a plan to burn down London so he might get some work rebuilding it.

The Industrial Revolution

WHEN? It began around the middle of
the 18th century.

WHERE? In the cities and towns of
England and Wales.

WHAT WAS THAT ALL ABOUT? The Industrial Revolution
was brought about by new inventions such as steam power.
Jobs which were once done by hand were now done by
machines. Labour shifted from agriculture to industry,
causing people to move from the countryside to the cities.
Improved transport was provided by canals, roads, railways
and steamships.

CHECK THIS OUT: In 1765 James Hargreaves invented an
improved spinning wheel called the 'spinning jenny'.
Spinners on the old-fashioned wheels were alarmed at the
threat to their employment. In 1768 a mob broke into
Hargreaves' house and destroyed the machinery.

AND THIS IS JUST WEIRD: The first railway opened in 1830
between Manchester and Liverpool. It travelled at thirty-five
miles an hour and second class carriages had no roof.

HUMUNGOUS HOAX

In 1761 James Brindley completed the Bridgewater Canal between Worsley and Manchester and then extended it to Liverpool in 1776. Many people believe that canals were built for transporting goods on barges – but this isn't actually the case. Canals were originally built for fish herding. Fish were driven in from the sea, down the canals in large shoals by special boats with a mesh on the front. The idea was to herd fish into the heart of all the cities all over Britain so that everyone could have fresh fish. This drawing by James Brindley shows the idea.

FISH CANALS TO HERD FRESH FISH
INTO THE HEART OF THE CITIES.

Napoleon Bonaparte

WHEN? Napoleon I (known as Napoleon Bonaparte before he became emperor) was born in 1769 and died in 1821.

WHERE? In France.

WHAT WAS THAT ALL ABOUT? Napoleon was emperor of France between 1804-14. A brilliant military leader, he tried to extend French rule over large areas of Europe. In the end, he was defeated by the Duke of Wellington and Gebhard von Blucher at the Battle of Waterloo in Belgium on 18th June 1815.

CHECK THIS OUT: In 1803 Napoleon got together an army of 170,000 ready to invade Britain, but it never quite happened because at that moment Austria resumed war with France.

AND THIS IS JUST WEIRD: In February 1804 a plot financed by Britain to assassinate Napoleon was uncovered by the former French police minister Joseph Fouche. Napoleon gave him his job back after that.

I think he meant the other sort of cannon.

HUMUNGOUS HOAX

Despite popular opinion, Napoleon was not really a short man. In fact, he was over seven feet tall, but was so embarrassed about his height, he went about on his knees with a specially made coat to cover them.

LE MANTEAU NOUVEAU POUR
GENERAL NAPOLEON BONAPARTE

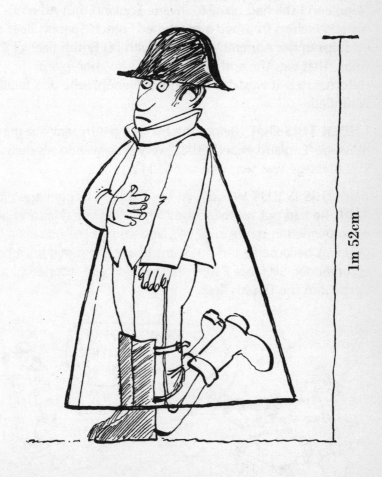

1m 52cm

FAST FACTS FILE
The Battle of Trafalgar

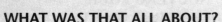

WHEN? The Battle of Trafalgar
took place on 21st October 1805.

WHERE? Trafalgar is on the
south west coast of Spain.

WHAT WAS THAT ALL ABOUT?

Napoleon I still had plans to invade England, but Admiral
Horatio Nelson smashed a combined French-Spanish fleet of
33 ships under Admiral Villeneuve with his British fleet of 27
ships. That was the end of Napoleon's invasion plans.
Unfortunately it was also the end of Nelson, who was fatally
wounded.

CHECK THIS OUT: Before the battle, Nelson sent out the
message 'England expects that every man will do his duty.'
The message was sent using coded flags.

AND THIS IS JUST WEIRD: At the Battle of Copenhagen in
1801, he had put his telescope to his blind eye (Nelson had
been blinded in battle in 1794), and said; "I see no signal."
This was because he did not want to see the signal from his
commander, Sir Hyde Parker that would have stopped him
destroying the Danish fleet.

HUMUNGOUS HOAX

Nelson never signalled his fleet using flags with the message 'England expects Every Man to Do His Duty.' It was his washing hanging out on the flagpole to dry. The document below proves it.

Dear Hardy,

Please hang out all my washing on the flagpole in the yard. I want to look smart for the Battle of Trafalgar. I seem to have a lot of underwear that needs doing. These are the pairs I would especially like clean.

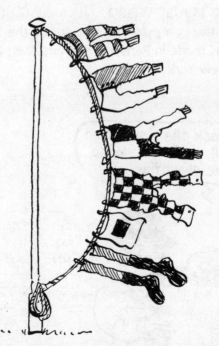

The Eiffel Tower

WHEN? The Eiffel Tower was
built in 1889.

WHERE? In Paris, France.

WHAT WAS THAT ALL ABOUT?
It was designed by the French structural
engineer Alexandre Gustave Eiffel for
the Paris Exhibition of 1889 to celebrate scientific and
engineering achievements of the age.

CHECK THIS OUT: It is a staggering 300 metres
(984 feet) tall.

AND THIS IS JUST WEIRD: Alexandre Gustave Eiffel also
designed the iron pylon support inside the Statue of Liberty,
which was made in Paris in 1884 and then transported by
ship to New York as a gift.

HUMUNGOUS HOAX

The Eiffel Tower in Paris was actually built as a TV aerial
for a small television company in the 1950s. It had to be
tall because the signal was so weak in those days.
These original plans have been discovered.

La nouvelle station TV de Paris -
March 17th 1956

Queen Victoria

WHEN? Born in 1819, Victoria reigned from 1837, until her death in 1901.

WHERE? She was queen of the United Kingdom.

WHAT WAS THAT ALL ABOUT? A popular queen, Victoria was the longest-reigning monarch in British history. She is famous for being stern, and for once saying: "We are not amused."

CHECK THIS OUT: Victoria was so upset when her husband Albert died in 1861 that she remained in mourning until her own death. She spent most of her time on the Isle of Wight or in the Scottish Highlands, where her closest companion was a dour Scottish servant, John Brown.

AND THIS IS JUST WEIRD: Victoria wore black from 1861 until her death.

HUMUNGOUS HOAX

After Albert died, Victoria wore black. She also pretended to be very sombre and reserved. However, she was having her own private joke that no one knew about until now. Underneath all those black dresses, Queen Victoria wore the most outrageously sparkly and colourful underwear. These are some sketches drawn by her designer of the clothes she wore that have only just come to light at the Victoria and Albert Museum in London.

Date: 15th September 1863.

*Underwear, petticoats and corsets for
Her Majesty Queen Victoria.*

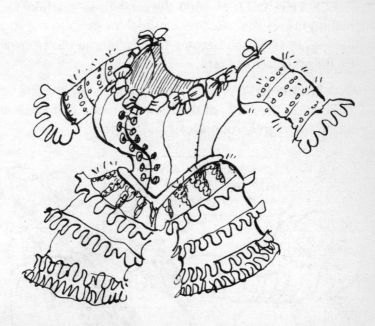

Florence Nightingale

WHEN? She was born in 1820 and died in 1910.

WHERE? Florence Nightingale was based at British army hospitals in Crimea. Crimea is in present day Ukraine on the Black Sea.

WHAT WAS THAT ALL ABOUT? The Crimean War was fought between Russia and an alliance of Britain, France, Sardinia and Turkey in 1853-56. Florence Nightingale was appointed supervisor of nursing at British army hospitals during the war. She is considered the founder of modern nursing and a pioneer of sanitation and hygiene.

CHECK THIS OUT: In 1860 she established a school for training nurses that became a model for modern nursing training. In 1907 she became the first woman to be awarded the British Order of Merit.

AND THIS IS JUST WEIRD: Her nickname among the soldiers was the 'Lady of the Lamp', a name that came about due to her nightly rounds carrying a light.

HUMUNGOUS HOAX

Florence Nightingale was not the only nurse out in the field caring for soldiers. She had a sister, but because she didn't have a lamp, no one knew she was there. This is the only portrait of her that survives, drawn by a soldier in his bunk.

Soon after this I did hear a lady cry "Oof- ah- my toe! Who left that bed there? Ow!"

HOAX TIPS (2)

After ageing the documents (see pages 22 and 94), there is still more you can do to make your chosen documents appear completely authentic.

- Put the document in a frame. This will make it look more important and stop the teacher examining the back of it too closely.

- Cover the frame in a little dust. This will help persuade your teacher that the document has been around for years. You can make dust by mixing some dry grey powder paint with some white flour. Then sieve it over the frame.

- Stick one of the labels printed on the opposite page to the back of the frame as a final touch. Let your teacher find it. They'll think they have discovered something that will make them want to believe it is all true. (You may want to age these labels with tea as well – see page 22.)

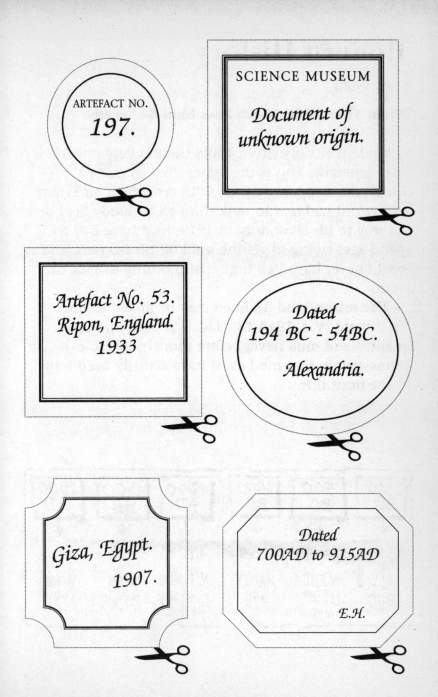

ARTEFACT NO.
197.

SCIENCE MUSEUM

*Document of
unknown origin.*

*Artefact No. 53.
Ripon, England.
1933*

*Dated
194 BC - 54BC.*

Alexandria.

*Giza, Egypt.
1907.*

*Dated
700AD to 915AD*

E.H.

Modern History

(from 1900)

When There Was Much Less Mud Generally.

In Modern History (from 1900) there is very much less mud generally. This is the reason that so many discoveries happened in the 20th century. If Sir Ernest Rutherford had had to walk through a muddy field on the way to his laboratory in 1919, he'd have had to spend ages trying to get the mud off his trousers, and would never have had time that morning to split the atom.

The reason mud declined may be linked to the First World War (1914-18). This war used up huge quantities of mud never before thought possible. It seems certain that mud must have actually been sent to the front line.

2000 BC — ALL MUD · 1500 BC — AN AWFUL LOT OF MUD · 1000 BC — MAINLY MUD · 1000 AD — NOT QUITE SO MUDDY · 1500 AD — MUDDY PATCHES · 2000 AD — NO MUD AT ALL

It appears that so much mud was sent to the front that the soldiers in the trenches were forced to live in it day after day. Wilfred Owen (1893-1918) was an English poet of the First World War, who, in his work recreated the bleak realism of the horrors of the war. However, he also wrote a lesser-known poem in which he recalls the bleak realism of the mud in the First World War.

Very little of this mud ever came home again after the war, so modern history is relatively mud free. Now people could finally get on with all the fiddly things that you can't do when your fingers are caked in soil. And this is the reason why no end of history has happened since 1900. For example, Einstein's Theory of Relativity (1912) which was quite fiddly, Picasso's Cubist painting (Guernica 1937), which had some fiddly bits to it, and sending men to the moon (1969) which was very fiddly indeed.

So, put on your space helmet! Sling on your Enfield rifle! Cover yourself in Chanel No 5! Modern history is upon us!

Note from the Editor:
Please note that the humorous 'mud theory' (see also pages 7 and 23) has been entirely made up by the author. There is no evidence to prove the theory – it merely represents the author's own hilarious way of thinking and interpreting!

Emily Pankhurst

WHEN? Emmeline Goulden Pankhurst was born in 1858 and died in 1928.

WHERE? England.

WHAT WAS THAT ALL ABOUT? In 1903 Emily founded the Women's Social and Political Union. She was joined by her two daughters, Christabel Harriette Pankhurst and Estelle Sylvia Pankhurst. They campaigned for women's voting rights and representation in Parliament.

CHECK THIS OUT: Their demonstrations were pretty extreme and they did things like burning letter boxes, assaulting prominent opponents and breaking windows. Not surprisingly, they were often arrested.

AND THIS IS JUST WEIRD: They also chained themselves to railings in Downing Street so they could not be easily removed.

HUMUNGOUS HOAX

The reason it took until 1918 for women to get full voting rights is shown in this voting slip used on the subject at the turn of the century (1903).

THE HOUSE OF COMMONS
VOTING SLIP
2nd March 1903

Should Women Have The Vote?

PLEASE TICK ONE BOX CLEARLY.

No. We can't have them worrying their pretty little heads. ☐

Women – they're the ones in the dresses aren't they? ☐

Don't be ridiculous – they don't know the first thing about cricket. ☐

I'd like another gin and tonic and then I want to hear no more about the subject. ☐

I mean really – honestly – can you see a woman being Prime Minister of the United Kingdom? ☐

Captain Scott

WHEN? Robert Falcon Scott was born in 1868 and died in 1912. He was an English naval officer and explorer who led the second expedition to reach the South Pole in 1910-12.

WHERE? The South Pole is in Antarctica.

WHAT WAS THAT ALL ABOUT? Scott wanted to be the first person to reach the South Pole ahead of his rival, the Norwegian Roald Amundsen. Scott took four companions to the Pole: Wilson, Oates, Bowers and Evans. The race captured the imagination of Europe.

CHECK THIS OUT: Scott's party reached the South Pole on 18th January 1912, only to find Amundsen had reached it a month earlier. Scott died of starvation and exposure on his journey back to base.

AND THIS IS JUST WEIRD: Amundsen left Scott a note at the South Pole.

HUMUNGOUS HOAX

The reason Scott didn't beat Amundsen to the South Pole was actually because he did not fully appreciate the conditions he was to encounter. This can be gleaned from his equipment list.

Robert Falcon Scott
Polar Explorer

5th January 1910

Supplementary itinerary for supplies and equipment for South Pole expedition 1910-12

Spare compass
Spare woollen hat (with bobble)
Spare over-boots
Snow goggles
Camera
Film
Skis
Ski wax
Après ski boots
Ice Skates
Ice hockey stick
Puck
Helmet
Ice Hockey shirt
Shoulder pads
Golf clubs? Ask Oates if he's taking his.

The Titanic

WHEN? The *Titanic*, a British passenger liner, sank on the night of 14th-15th April 1912.

WHERE? It hit a big iceberg off Newfoundland, in the Atlantic Ocean.

WHAT WAS THAT ALL ABOUT? The *Titanic* was the largest and most luxurious liner built up to that time. The White Star Line vessel was on her maiden (very first) voyage from Southampton, England to New York. She was supposed to be 'unsinkable'.

CHECK THIS OUT: *Titanic* took about two hours and forty minutes to sink after hitting the iceberg.

AND THIS IS JUST WEIRD: She was carrying more than 2,200 people. About 1,500 drowned including the radio operator who stayed at his post, and the band who carried on playing as she sank.

I couldn't find the emergency rockets, Captain – but I did find some Catherine wheels. Pretty, aren't they?

HUMUNGOUS HOAX

This is the proof the radio operator stayed at his post.
The last message sent from the 'S.S. Titanic' was
a telegram.

Wireless Message

S. 7448d

Time received.	Operator.	Priority
1.50a.m.	G. Jones	High

From: S.S. Titanic. 15th April 1912

S.O.S. We are sinking. Help.
Immediately. We are sinking. S.O.S.
Splooooooooooooosh. Glug glug glug glug
glug glug glug. Hello fish. Wooo — it's
dark. Glug... glug... glug.

First World War Armistice

WHEN? It was signed at 5.00 am
on 11th November 1918. First World
War hostilities ceased at 11.00 am
on the same day.

WHERE? In a railway coach on a
siding at Compiegne, northern France.

WHAT WAS THAT ALL ABOUT? The railway coach was the
headquarters of Ferdinand Foch, the Allied commander-in-
chief. The terms specified that the German army must
immediately evacuate all occupied territory and give up all
their war machinery such as submarines and warships.

CHECK THIS OUT: The German delegation who signed the
armistice was led by a civilian (a person not in the armed
forces) called Matthias Erzberger.

AND THIS IS JUST WEIRD: During the war, on Christmas
Day 1915, German and British soldiers came out of the
trenches and met in 'no-man's land' where they chatted and
played football. The next day they went back to shooting
each other again.

That's a terrible tackle. Someone's going to get badly hurt out there.

HUMUNGOUS HOAX

The armistice at the end of the First World War was signed on a train. This is the original copy. As you can see, it was a bit difficult to write neatly with the train moving along. Because it was unreadable, many people think the confusion led directly to the Second World War, several years later.

ARMISTICE AGREEMENT

on this day
November 11th 1918,

between

Matthias Erzberger
empowered as head of the German delegation

and

Ferdinand Foch
Allied commander-in-chief.

This agreement duly signed below

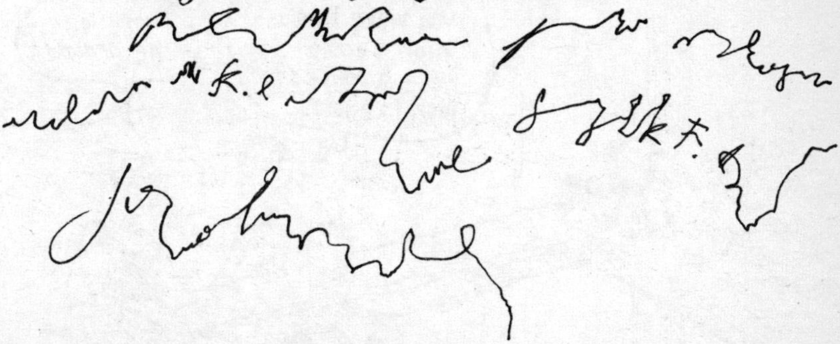

FAST FACTS FILE

Empire State Building

WHEN? It was built in 1930-31.

WHERE? Fifth Avenue in
New York City, USA.

WHAT WAS THAT ALL ABOUT?
At the time it was the tallest
building in the world, at
381 metres (1,250 feet).

CHECK THIS OUT: The building
was opened during the great
Depression (when the USA and
some other countries had money problems) and much of its
floor space remained empty for ages.

AND THIS IS JUST WEIRD: Native American Indians were
employed to help build the structure because they weren't
afraid to walk along the narrow steel girders hundreds of feet
in the air.

HUMUNGOUS HOAX

It was not meant to be the tallest building in the world.
The plans for two separate buildings, The Empire Building
and The State Building got stuck together.

THE EMPIRE
BUILDING

THE STATE
BUILDING

The London Blitz

WHEN? The Blitz on London occurred in 1940, during the Second World War.

WHERE? To begin with, it was just the East End of London that was bombed but soon the whole of London came under attack.

WHAT WAS THAT ALL ABOUT? As part of his attack on Britain, the German leader Adolf Hitler decided to try and break the morale of ordinary British people by sending the Luftwaffe (German Airforce) to bomb London night after night. Although it caused mass devastation and many people lost their lives, the spirit of the British people did not die.

CHECK THIS OUT: Sixty thousand people slept in the tube stations every night. Many others built shelters in their gardens called 'Anderson Shelters'. Others decided to risk it and stayed in the comfort of their own beds.

AND THIS IS JUST WEIRD: In 1944 the Germans invented the V1 flying bomb and fired these at London. When these V1s ran out of fuel they fell out of the sky. They were nicknamed 'Buzz Bombs' or 'Doodlebugs'.

The way I see it, Mr Doodlebug, you'll only get hit by one if it's got your name on it.

HUMUNGOUS HOAX

Not many people know that Winston Churchill invented 'cockneys' to help keep morale high during the bombing raids in East London. They were trained at a top secret cockney training school, then housed in the East End and filmed for news reports. Here is an original timetable from the training school.

TIMETABLE

	9.15–10am	10–10.45am	Break	11.15–12pm
Monday	Cockney rhyming slang	Being chirpy		Drinking tea with lots of sugar
Tuesday	Saying 'cor blimey guv'	Cheerfulness		Selling fruit on a stall
Wednesday	Cockney rhyming slang	Being chipper		Cheekiness
Thursday	Advanced cheerfulness	Cockney rhyming slang		Being chirpy
Friday	Singing cheerful songs	Drinking tea with lots of sugar		Having a grubby face and smiling

---

Evacuation

WHEN? 1939-45, during
World War II.

WHERE? Evacuation happened
in London and many other cities in England.

WHAT WAS THAT ALL ABOUT? Evacuation is the removal
of people from a place of danger to a safe place. The war
office decided to evacuate children from the main cities to
the countryside. In 1939 about half of London's children
were evacuated and lived with other families outside London.

CHECK THIS OUT: Their parents could visit them at
weekends, but because no bombs fell on London until
September 1940, many parents took their children back
home again. When the Blitz began, a new wave of
evacuation started.

AND THIS IS JUST WEIRD: It wasn't just children who left
the cities. The population in Folkestone in Kent went down
from 46,000 to just 6,000. All the animals from London Zoo
were evacuated and many of London's oldest trees were dug
up and moved.

HUMUNGOUS HOAX

As well as children, adults, animals and trees, there were even plans to evacuate many of London's most famous buildings to save them from the bombs. Evidence is provided in the form of this memo, although the plans were never actually carried out.

HOME  OFFICE

WHITEHALL S.W.1

MEMO

Mr. Stephen Lee, of Pullam St. Mary in Suffolk has said he has enough land to accept the store Harrods for the duration of the war. Please have this dismantled and rebuilt on his land as soon as possible. He has asked for it to be positioned near the cow sheds and covered in a large tarpaulin. Details to follow.

Sir Timothy Twisten

Home Office Minister

FAST FACTS FILE

Neil Armstrong

WHEN? Neil Alden Armstrong was born on August 5th 1930.

WHERE? Wapakoneta in Ohio, USA.

WHAT WAS THAT ALL ABOUT?
Neil Armstrong was the first man on the moon, on 30th July 1969. As he stepped off the ladder he said: "That's one small step for (a) man, one giant leap for mankind." NASA (National Aeronautics and Space Administration) later said that the word 'a' had been lost in the radio transmission.

CHECK THIS OUT: He had been a test pilot at Edwards Air Force base and flown the X-15 rocket plane seven times.

AND THIS IS JUST WEIRD: Armstrong received his pilot's licence on his 16th birthday.

HUMUNGOUS HOAX

What was actually in those bulky white backpacks they wore on the moon? It was supposed to be scientific instruments, but as this picture shows, Neil Armstrong broke NASA rules and packed his with things he really wanted.

neck support

hat

football

travel chess

wine gums

dressing gown

tapes

travel scrabble

HOAX TIPS (3)

Background story

With most of these documents you'll need a background story to explain how you came to have them. You could say you had a distant relative who used to be an archaeologist. They travelled the world and passed down all sorts of things to your family and they're in boxes in the roof. (The artefacts that is – not the relative.)

These are the sort of questions your teacher may ask and here are a few answers to help you. Your background story must be foolproof. If they smell a rat – the hoax will not work.

Where did you get this from?

Found it in the roof / my mum was left it / picked it up at a car boot sale / we've had it for years / I think we were given it by a relative / I stepped through a freak hole in the space time continuum and found it lying about. (This last one is actually pretty tricky to pull off.)

What did your relative do?

My uncle was an archaeologist / my grandfather travelled the world with the army / my aunt married a diplomat and was posted all over the word / my grandfather was in Egypt during the war.

These are just a few ideas. It's much better to make up your own story. It is most important to keep a straight face when presenting your hoax to the teacher. I cannot stress this enough.

Good luck.

APPENDIX

All good history books have appendices. 'Appendix' roughly translates as: 'Oh there's another thing we must put in.'

Hoax Badges

If you do manage to hoax your teacher you may like to cut out and wear one of these badges. This will serve to remind the class and teacher of the glorious moment. Don't wear them for too long however, as it's only cool to push the point home for a day or two.

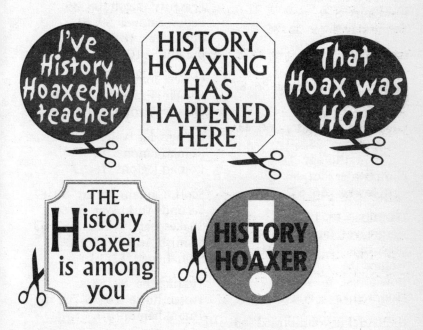

To make your badge, choose which one you'd like to wear, cut it out and stick it to a piece of cardboard. Then stick a safety pin to the reverse.

INDEX